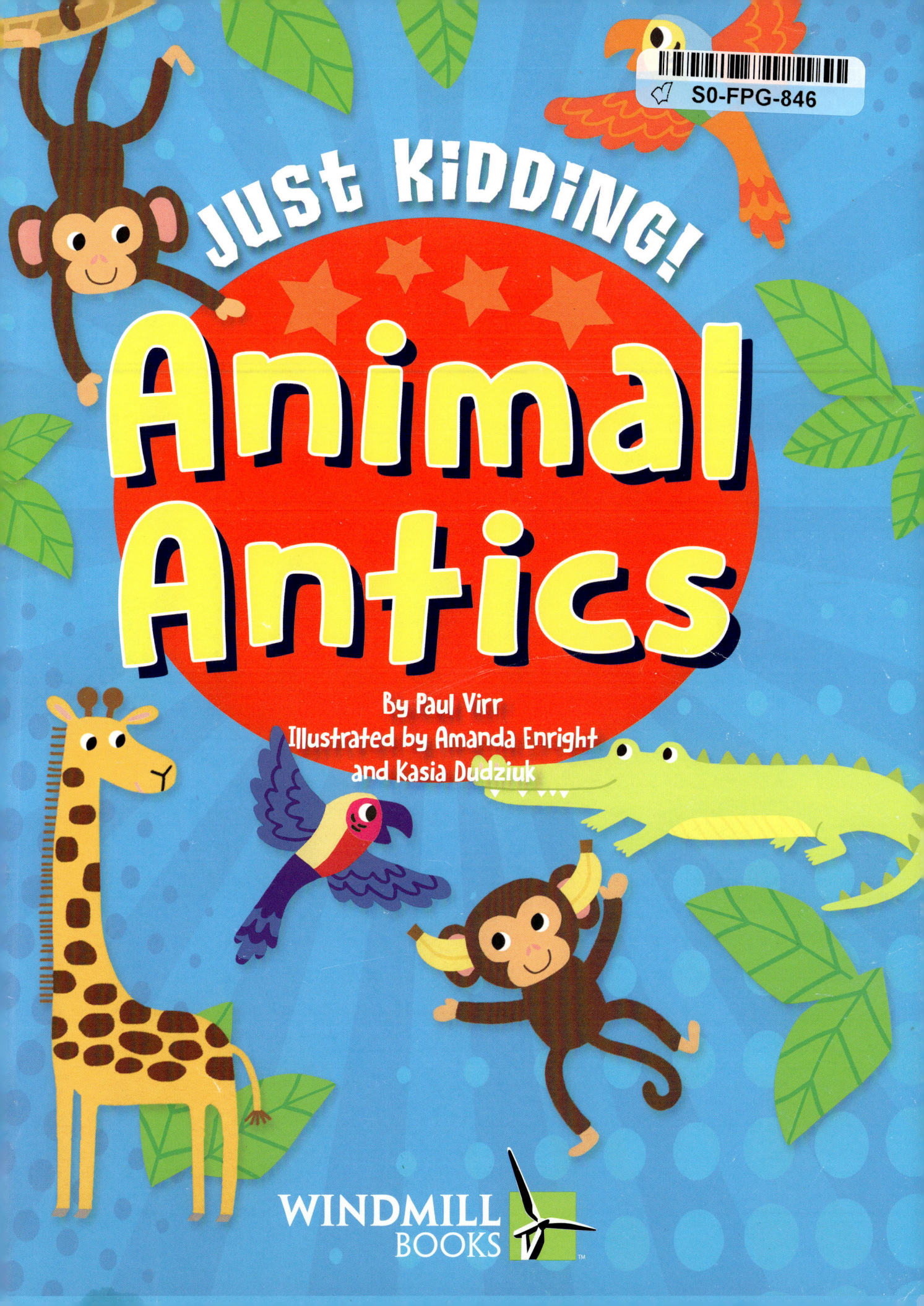

Just Kidding!
Animal Antics

By Paul Virr
Illustrated by Amanda Enright
and Kasia Dudziuk

WINDMILL BOOKS

Published in 2020 by Windmill Books,
an Imprint of Rosen Publishing
29 East 21st Street, New York, NY 10010

Copyright © Arcturus Holdings Ltd, 2020

All rights reserved. No part of this book may be reproduced in any form without permission in writing from the publisher, except by a reviewer.

Cataloging-in-Publication Data

Names: Virr, Paul.
Title: Animal antics / Paul Virr.
Description: New York : Windmill Books, 2020. | Series: Just kidding! | Includes glossary and index.
Identifiers: ISBN 9781725393004 (pbk.) | ISBN 9781538391204 (library bound) | ISBN 9781538391198 (6 pack)
Subjects: LCSH: Animals--Juvenile humor. | Wit and humor, Juvenile. | Riddles, Juvenile.
Classification: LCC PN6231.A5 V577 2019 | DDC 818'.602 --dc23

Manufactured in the United States of America

CPSIA Compliance Information: Batch BS19WM: For Further Information contact Rosen Publishing, New York, New York at 1-800-237-9932

Contents

Funny Bunnies!...4

Silly Dinosaur Jokes...6

Hopping Mad!..10

What a Hoot!...12

Snake School..14

Crazy Cats!...16

Zany Zoo...18

Dippy Dogs..20

Feeding Time!..22

All at Sea!...24

Mischievous Mice..28

Totally Quackers!...30

Glossary, Index...32

Funny Bunnies!

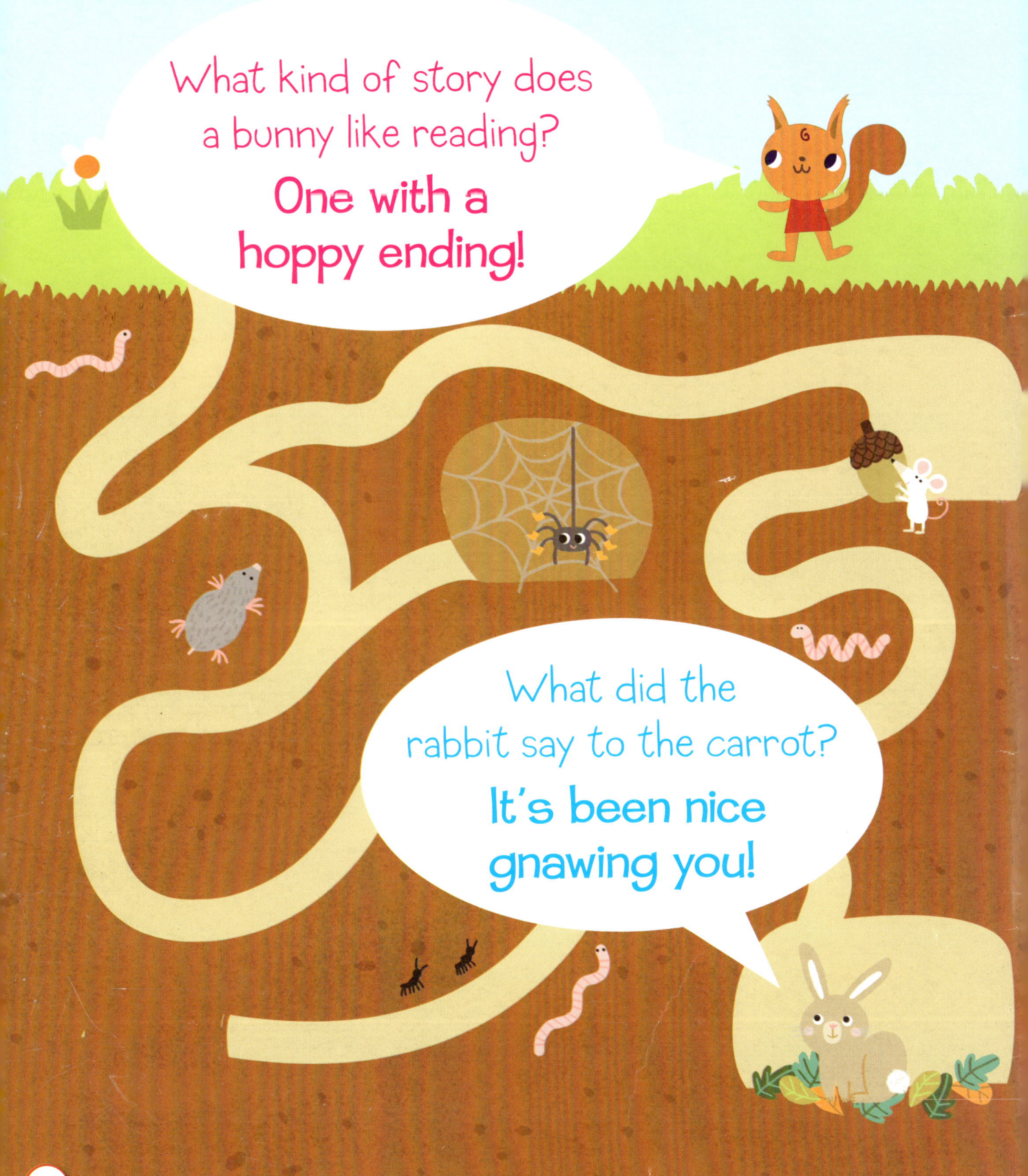

What kind of story does a bunny like reading? **One with a hoppy ending!**

What did the rabbit say to the carrot? **It's been nice gnawing you!**

Are carrots good for your eyesight? Have you ever seen a bunny wearing glasses?

Why did the rabbit wear a hat? She was having a bad hare day!

Silly Dinosaur Jokes

What do you call a dinosaur with poor eyesight?
Doyouthinkhesaurus!

Which dinosaur keeps all the others awake at night?
Bronto-snore-us!

What has three horns and sixteen wheels?

A Triceratops on roller skates!

Which dinosaur can't go out in the rain?
A Stegosaur-rust!

Hopping Mad!

What kind of candy do kangaroos like?
Lolli-hops!

What do you get if you cross a snake with a kangaroo?
A jump rope!

Can a kangaroo hop higher than a house? **Yes—houses can't hop!**

What do you call a tired kangaroo? **Out of bounds!**

What a Hoot!

What do you call an angry owl?
A gr-owl!

How do birds keep fit?
They eggs-ercise!

What is more amazing than a talking owl? **A spelling bee!**

Did you hear about the owl that had a sore throat? **It couldn't give a hoot!**

Snake School

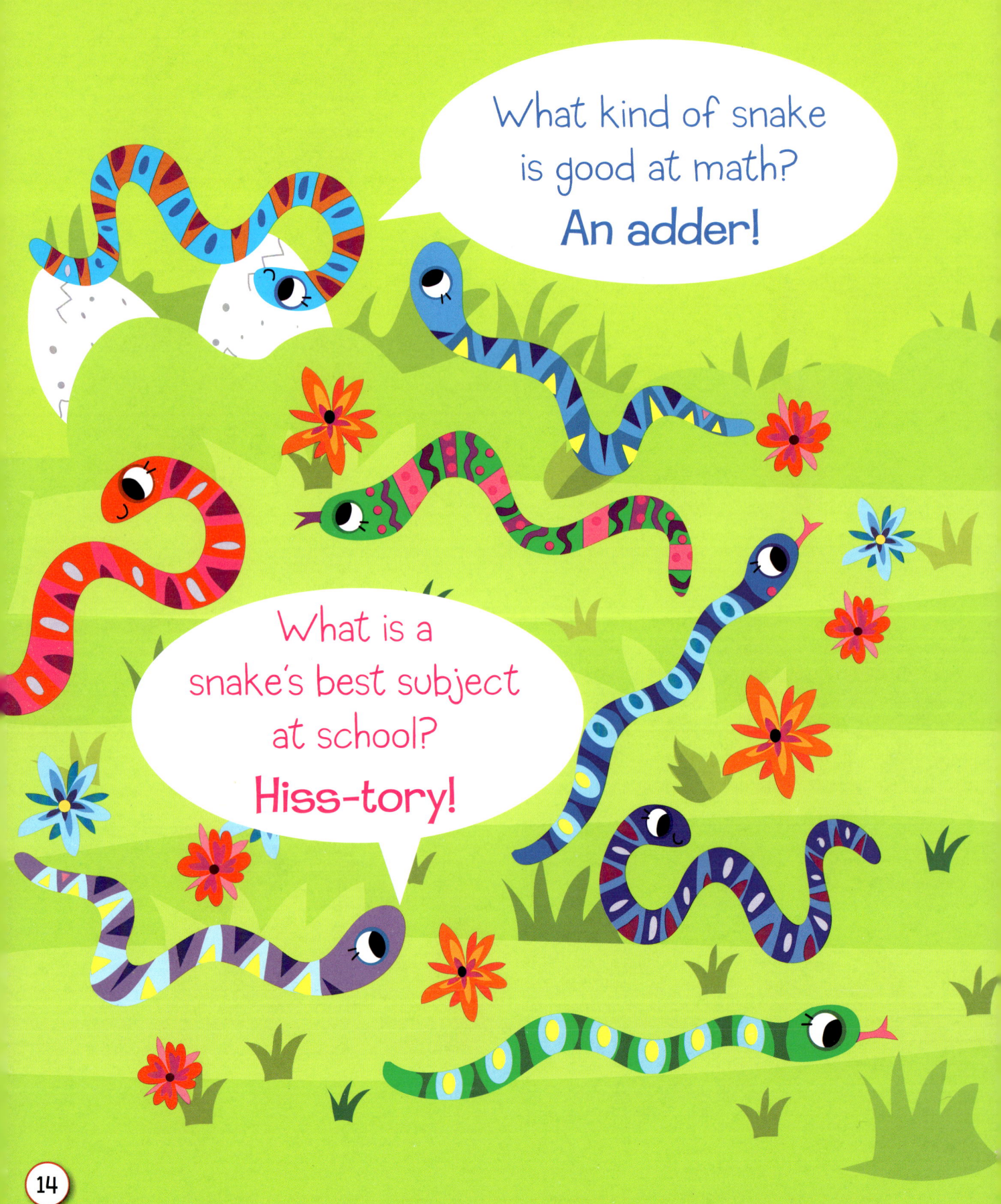

What kind of snake is good at math?
An adder!

What is a snake's best subject at school?
Hiss-tory!

How can you tell that a snake is a baby?
It has a rattle!

Why is it hard to trick a snake?
You can't pull its leg!

Crazy Cats!

What do you call a young cat that becomes a doctor?
A first aid kitty!

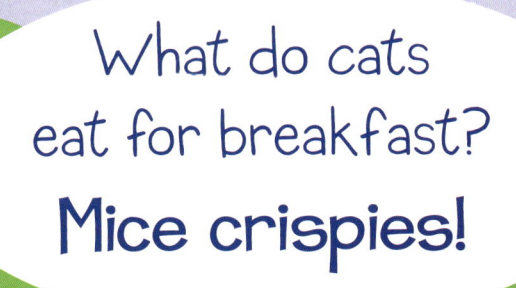

What do cats eat for breakfast?
Mice crispies!

Where did the kittens go on their school trip?
A meow-seum!

Which game do cats like to play with mice?
Catch!

Zany Zoo

What do penguins love to eat?
Ice-burgers!

Why did the tiger follow the lion?
He was a copycat!

What do you call a lion with an elephant standing on his tail? **Rory!**

Why do giraffes have such long legs? **Because their feet smell!**

Dippy Dogs

Did you hear about the dog that could tell the time? **It was a watchdog!**

Why was the dog scratching after it went shopping? **It had been to a flea market!**

Which dog has the shiniest fur?
A sham-poodle!

Where did the dog fall asleep?
In the barking lot!

Feeding Time!

How often do lions eat?
They have just one mane meal a day!

What's the worst day of the week to meet a hungry tiger?
Chewsday!

Why is it so cheap to feed a giraffe?
Because a little food goes a long way!
Which fruit do gorillas like the best?
Ape-ricots!

All at Sea!

Why did the shark blush?
It saw the ship's bottom!

What do you call a baby whale?
A little squirt!

Why did the jellyfish cross the ocean?
To get to the other tide!

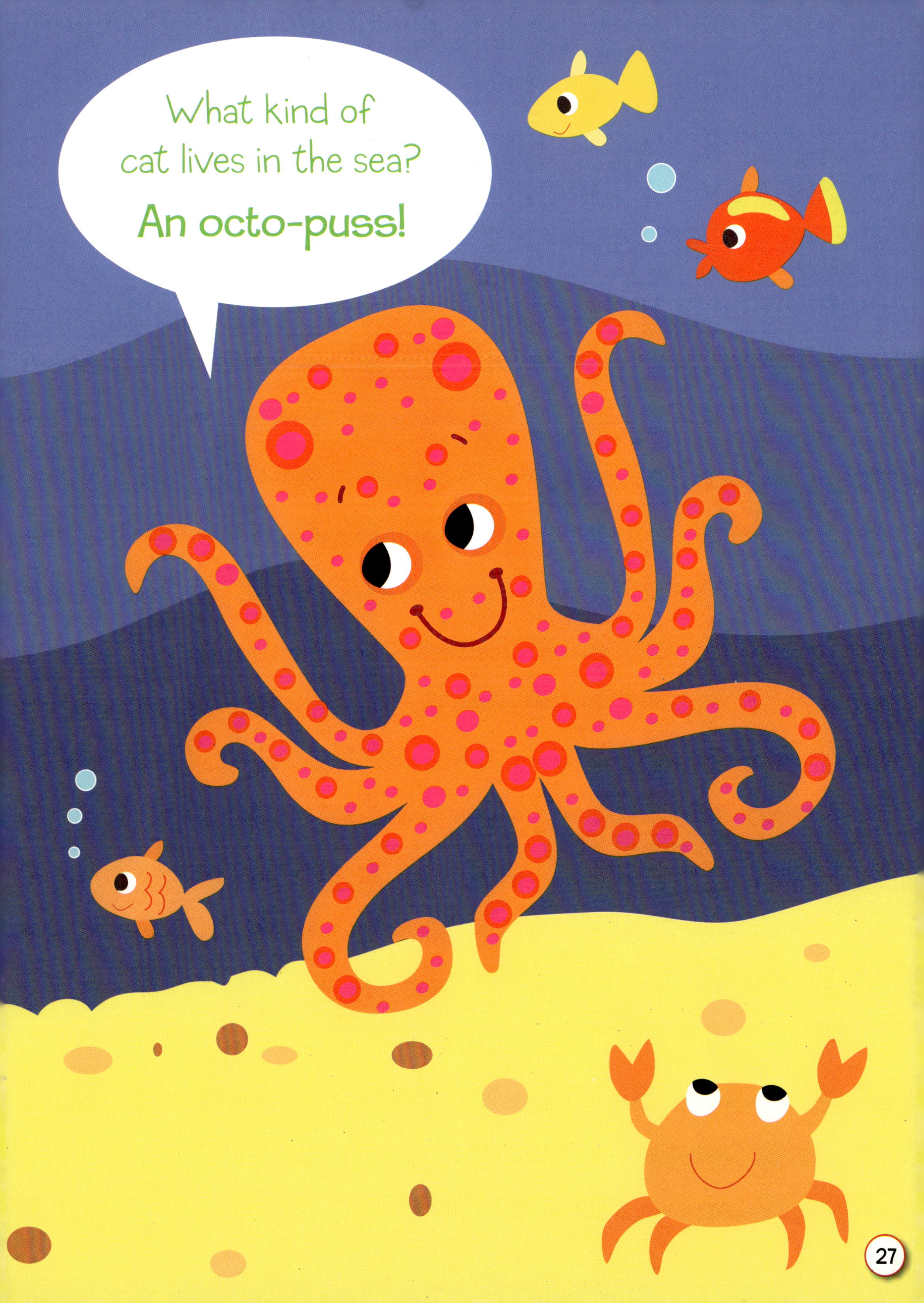
What kind of cat lives in the sea?
An octo-puss!

Mischievous Mice

How do you make a mouse smile?
Ask it to say cheese!

Why are mice so tidy?
They always do the mouse-work.

What are small, furry, and carry swords?
The three mouse-keteers!

What do angry mice send at Christmas?
Cross-mouse cards!

Totally Quackers!

What time does a duck wake up?
The quack of dawn!

Where did the duck go when she was sick?
To the duck-tor!

What do ducks watch on TV? **Duck-umentaries!**

What did the duck do when it heard a joke? **It quacked up!**

Glossary

first aid Emergency care or treatment.
gnawing Biting or chewing.
mane Long hair that grows from the neck of some animals.
tide The rising and falling of the surface of the ocean.
watchdog A dog kept to guard a house.

Index

A
adders 14

B
birds 12-13

C
cats 16-17

D
dinosaurs 6-9
dogs 20-21
ducks 30-31

G
giraffes 19, 23

J
jellyfish 26

K
kangaroos 10-11

L
lions 19, 22

M
mice 28-29

O
octopus 27
owls 12-13

P
penguins 18

R
rabbits 4-5
roller skates 8

S
school 14
sea 24-27
shark 24
snakes 14-15
Stegosaurus 9

T
tigers 18, 22
Triceratops 8

W
whale 25

Z
zebras 18
zoo 18-19